Living Stories

Godı Weghàà Ets' eèda

Fifth House Ltd.
A Fitzhenry & Whiteside Company
195 Allstate Parkway
Markham, Ontario L3R 4T8
1-800-387-9776
www.fitzhenry.ca

The Canada Council | Le Conseil des Arts
FOR THE ARTS | DU CANADA
SINCE 1957 | DEPUIS 1957

CANADIAN NORTH
seriously northern

CIBC

Northwest
Territories Education, Culture and Employment

FSC

Mixed Sources
Product group from well-managed
forests and other controlled sources
www.fsc.org Cert no. SW-COC-1271
© 1996 Forest Stewardship Council

First published in the
United States in 2009 by
Fitzhenry & Whiteside
311 Washington Street
Brighton, Massachusetts,
02135

Royalties from *Living Stories* are put back into the *The Land is Our Storybook* series and shared between the authors. For simplicity, as there are many authors, copyright is held by Mindy WIllett (co-author and series coordinator), but the contract clearly outlines that all authors remain in control of how their stories are used. For more information, please contact Fifth House Publishers.

Cover and interior design by John Luckhurst
Frontispiece map by Toby Foord
Photography by Tessa Macintosh
Additional photographs by Tapwe Chretien, Native Communications Society
(drum-dance circle, p. 6), Mindy Willett (feeding the fire, p. 11), Mindy Willett
(Elizabeth's hands folding basket, p. 15), Richard Finnie/NWT Archives/N–1979–063–0047
(Chief Jimmy Bruneau, p. 16), Miles Griffin, CJBS (graduating class of 2008, p. 16).
Edited by Meaghan Craven
Proofread by Ann Sullivan

The type in this book is set in 10-on-15 point Trebuchet Regular and 10-on-13 point Tekton Oblique.

The publisher gratefully acknowledges the support of The Canada Council for the Arts and the Department of Canadian Heritage.

We acknowledge the financial support of the Government of Canada through the Book Publishing Industry Development Program (BPIDP) for our publishing activities.

The author would like to thank the NWT Protected Areas Strategy Secretariat, CIBC, WWF-Canada, Canadian North, and the Tłı̨chǫ government for financial assistance in the completion of this book.

Printed in Canada by Friesens on Forest Stewardship Council (FSC) approved paper

2009 / 1

Library and Archives Canada Cataloguing in Publication

Zoe, Therese, 1948-
Living stories / Therese Zoe, Philip Zoe and Mindy Willett.

Includes index.
ISBN 978-1-897252-44-4

1. Tlicho First Nation—History—Juvenile literature.
2. Dogrib Indians—Juvenile literature.
I. Willett, Mindy, 1968- II. Zoe, Philip, 1925- III. Title.

E99.T4Z63 2009   j971.9'3004972   C2008-906225-6

Acknowledgements

We would like to thank Dr. John B. Zoe, Tłįchǫ executive officer and cultural advocate, for his incredible support, guidance, leadership, and advice. Dr. John B. Zoe edited a book called *Trails of Our Ancestors: Building a Nation*, which helped us to write the information about Yamǫ̀ǫ̀zha that appears on page 19. We would also like to thank Tom Andrews of the Prince of Wales Heritage Centre; Kristy Cameron, John Stewart, and Gladys Norwegian for their reviews of the manuscript; Stanley Gon for helping us net fish; Chief Henry Gon, William and Camilla Chocolate, Therese and Gary Bekale, and others from the community of Gamètì for sharing their stories, dry-meat, and generally making us feel welcome. We would also like to thank Madelaine Chocolate, Tłįchǫ Knowledge and Language Researcher, and Allice Legat, former research director of the Tłįchǫ Regional Elders Committee. These two women worked with Elders from the four Tłįchǫ communities, and we are indebted to them for passing on the wishes of the Elders. Thanks to Mary Rose Sundberg for translations. The authors are also grateful for the support provided by: the staff at the Prince of Wales Heritage Museum; Dianne Lafferty for her wisdom and encouragement for the project; Fifth House publisher Charlene Dobmeier, promotions director Lyn Cadence, and editor Meaghan Craven; and Pete Ewins of WWF-Canada for his unwavering support. We would like to acknowledge June Helm and Nancy Lurie, whose text "The Dogrib Hand Game," published by the National Museum of Canada, helped in writing about the Tłįchǫ tea dance on page 6. A heartfelt thanks also goes to George Blondin for sharing his knowledge on storytelling and much more.

A project like this takes many people, including the support of family. We would like to thank: Tessa Macintosh's children, Oree and Alex Wah-Shee, who are proud to be a part of the Tłįchǫ Nation; Mindy's family, Damian, Jack, and Rae Panayi, for being so understanding when she's gone; Therese's family, especially her husband, Louis, and children, Nelson and Nancy, for helping, and Francis for allowing his children to participate, as well as her grandchildren, Adam, Nicole, Bradley, and Forest, who worked hard and were open to learning; Philip's family, including his son, Peter, and his daughter, Camilla, as well as his granddaughter, Shelinda, for being so mature and listening so intently to the words of her Elders; and especially Philip's sister, Elizabeth Chocolate, who always gave so much of herself and shared her knowledge and skills willingly.

This book is dedicated to the memory
of our Elder, Elizabeth Chocolate, who
died shortly after the pictures for this
book were taken. She loved being on
the land and doing all of our traditions.
She loved to come to our camp and
make dry-fish. She taught us a lot
and we really miss her.

Asìi łǫ hoghàgohtǫ Eyıts'ǫ
wekaneèts' èʔà.

Living Stories

Godı Weghàà Ets' eèda

By **THERESE ZOE,**
PHILIP ZOE *and*
MINDY WILLETT
Photographs by **Tessa Macintosh**

FIFTH
HOUSE

Yukon Territory

Northwest Territories

Arctic Circle

Nunavut

British Columbia

Labrador and Newfoundland

Alberta

Manitoba

Quebec

Prince Edward Island

Saskatchewan

Ontario

New Brunswick

Nova Scotia

Great Bear Lake

NWT   Nunavut

★ Gamètì

Wekwètì

Whatì

Behchokǫ̀

Mǫnfwì Lands
Tłı̨chǫ Land Area
Idaa Trail / Ìdàà tı̨lıı
Highway 3

Yellowknife

Great
Slave
Lake

Mackenzie River

Elizabeth Chocolate's caribou hide blanket provides the background to this page. She made the blanket from eighty strips of hide that came from caribou legs, from the knee to the ankle bone.

Edàt'e,

My name is Therese Zoe. I want to tell you some stories, but they are not my stories—they are Philip Zoe's and Elizabeth Chocolate's stories, Tłįchǫ stories.

Long ago the Tłįchǫ were very strong. Our medicines and stories were strong. After many years of contact with outsiders we have lost a lot of our culture, but not everything. In this book we want to share what our lives are like today and how we are using modern technology together with our traditions to stay healthy.

To us, being healthy means being mindful of self, others, animals, the land, and the spirit world. I'll share with you how we are holding on to our traditions and culture while we embrace the modern world. In doing so, our children can make healthy choices for their future and be, in the words of our Elders, strong like two people: *Dǫ Nàke Laanì Nàts'etso.*

These stories have many tellers. You'll meet some of my family, including my husband's brother and sister, Philip Zoe and Elizabeth Chocolate. They only speak Tłįchǫ, so I'll translate for you. To make this book, we worked together.

As you read about our ways, be respectful. These stories are sacred to us.

Masì Cho.

X   *Therese Zoe*

Philip Zoe   Therese Zoe

1

I live in Gamètì.

Gamètì was named after the Elder, Gamè, who lived on this land. Our small community of three hundred has a store, school, hotel and restaurant, airstrip, fire station, church, band office, health centre, winter ice road to Yellowknife, and even a golf course.

Many Gamètì houses are made of logs, and most people have a smokehouse tipi in their yards to make bogǫǫ̀ (dry-meat).

Philip, his son, Peter, and Therese sit together and have a cup of tea.

Gamètì is on a peninsula at the south end of a large island 177 kilometres northwest of Yellowknife, along a chain of waterways that Tłı̨chǫ people have used for hunting and travelling for thousands of years. It is called the Ɂdaà Trail. The trail connects Great Slave Lake to Great Bear Lake.

Bradley and Forest Zoe are Therese's grandsons.

Our Words

bogǫ̀ — dry meat

ehtsèe — grandfather

tì — lake or water, as in Gamètì

Therese makes bannock with her granddaughter, Nicole.

Philip is Shelinda's ehtsèe She is picking fireweed near the lakeshore.

In 2003, the Tłı̨chǫ Nation signed a modern-day treaty called a land claim agreement with the governments of Canada and the Northwest Territories. The agreement is very important to us, the Tłı̨chǫ people.

We are the fourth in the Northwest Territories to sign a land claim, but we are the first to have self-government. This means that, for the first time since we signed treaty in 1921, we have the right to take care of ourselves and make our own decisions about our lives. Now we can pass laws and make decisions that protect our language and culture among other things. We can run our child and family service programs, and we can set up rules about fishing and hunting. We also have a share of the money that comes from resource development, such as mining, on our lands.

The Tłı̨chǫ celebrate with a drum-dance when they gather. Philip is dancing in Behchokǫ̀. The hand-drum is the heart of the Tłı̨chǫ Nation. The dancers move in the same direction as the rising and setting sun, from east to west.

The Tłı̨chǫ assembly is made up of elected chiefs, councillors, and the grand chief.

We are all very proud of our self-government agreement. Our leaders had been working toward this since Chief Mǫnfwì signed Treaty 11 in 1921.

We now look forward to our future.

Bradley's future is bright. He's part of a proud, self-governing nation that can determine its own future.

Our Flag

The Tłı̨chǫ flag has four symbols.

1. The royal blue background represents the Tłı̨chǫ territory.
2. The tents represent the four Tłı̨chǫ Nation communities—Bechokǫ̀, Whatì, Gamètì and Wekweètì.
3. The sunrise and flowing river remind the people of the treaty that the great Chief Mǫnfwì signed.
4. The North Star is a hopeful symbol of a new era in which Tłı̨chǫ people can choose their own future. The star also shows Tłı̨chǫ commitment to protecting their language, culture, and way of life for future generations.

When Chief Mǫhkwì signed Treaty 11, he said:

"Dıı sah nàét'à. Dii deh nı̨ı̨lı̨. Dıı ndè nàgoèdǫ-le nı̨dè. Asıı ts'àgoèt' ǫ hǫlı̨ ha nele."

"As long as the sun shines and the river flows and the land does not change, we will not be restricted from our way of life."

Each summer the Tłįchǫ people have a gathering in one of our communities. We all meet and people get the chance to voice their opinions and plan the direction we should take. Every four years we elect our grand chief at this gathering, too. It's a time to be together, to dance, feast, and connect with each other.

Many people paddle to the community where the gathering will be held. The journeys to the gatherings are called "In the Trails of our Ancestors."

Right: Elders and youth restore old gravesites along the trail. Elders tell stories about who is buried there. In this way, youth are reminded about how their ancestors lived on the land.

The tea dance has no drums and only male singers. The dancers gather into an ever widening circle, moving with little steps from east to west. People dance tightly together facing into the centre of the circle. The name comes from the early days when the Hudson's Bay Company provided the chief with tea and bannock to share with the people who came into the fort with their winter's worth of fur.

Ancestral Trails

*T*he Tłįchǫ people use traditional trails all year long. They help people travel to areas where they have traditionally harvested food—meat, berries, and fish. The trails are alive with stories as each place name holds memories of important events in Tłįchǫ history. In this way, Tłįchǫ culture is tied to the landscape.

When travelling the trail, the people stop at each new waterway to make offerings of valuable items. In modern times people offer matches, coins, ammunition, or tobacco. The offering is a way of asking for good weather, food from the land, and safe travel. The Tłįchǫ also leave offerings at significant (or teaching) sites, such as places where ancestors are buried.

The people teach their children the stories of each of these important places and the stories teach the children about all aspects of Tłįchǫ life.

Dr. John B. Zoe is Tłįchǫ executive officer. He is dedicated to preserving, reviving, and celebrating the culture and language of the Tłįchǫ people. Here he is in his element, on the land with Elders and youth.

For many years, I have worked at the health centre in Gamètì as the community health representative (CHR). I help the nurses and translate for the Elders. I often provide health care when there is no nurse in our community.

I also explain our traditions and culture to the nurses because sometimes they don't understand our ways. For example, nurses want to clip new babies' fingernails, while our Elders teach that if babies' fingernails are clipped they won't have good luck when they grow up.

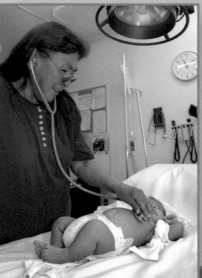

There is no regular doctor in Gamètì. Northern nurses are trained to deal with many different situations, like delivering babies in emergencies. To see a doctor, people must travel by plane to Yellowknife.

Before there was a health centre or nurse in Gamètì, Therese was the lay dispenser—she handed out prescription medicines to people. Although she has no formal training, she learned on the job and has been the community health representative for sixteen years.

Before health centres, we had medicine people. They were our doctors. They did not all have the same ability; some had more healing power than others. Today our Tłı̨chǫ medicine is not used as often as it once was, but some people still seek out traditional healers.

Medicine Person
Įk'ǫ̀ǫ̀ dǫ

As told by Philip Zoe

In those days a medicine person, įk'ǫ̀ǫ̀ dǫ could help a sick person in many different ways. He might put the sick person in front of him and put one hand on him and be very quiet or hum or sing. His humming and singing would get louder and louder. Then he would ask the sick person what was bothering him. The sick person needed to tell the medicine person what he wanted done with this illness. Should the medicine person throw it away, burn it, or swallow it? The medicine person would do what was instructed with the illness, and the person would get better. The medicine person would be strong enough to take the sickness into himself and yet not become ill.

Philip tells and shows the children what a medicine person would have done to cure a sick person in the old days. He makes the children feel welcome to share what he tells them with others.

Healers work in our community to help people stay healthy throughout their lives. Some people use sweat lodges or undertake fasts to heal their minds and bodies. We also use traditional plants as medicine.

Rat root, called *dzǫdii*, is a special plant for the Tłįchǫ people. We carry it with us for protection, especially when we're travelling. It helps us to have safe travels. It's a powerful plant.

You can burn rat root and the smell from it can cure a headache. If you have stomach cramps, chewing rat root will help ease the pain. When you use rat root as a medicine, you can't mix it with any other medicine. You also have to talk to the rat root, tell it what kind of help or healing you need, before you use it, or it won't work.

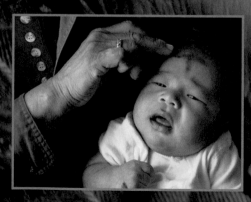

When Therese's grandson, Adam, is crying, she takes some ashes from the woodstove and makes a sign of the cross on his forehead to soothe him.

Our culture teaches us to be respectful and follow certain traditions. The traditions remind us of who we are and where we come from.

When we use fire, both at home and at drum-dances, we give it tea, bannock, dry-meat, matches, or something else that is important to us. By putting these things into the fire, we are feeding the fire: *Kǫ Ghàts´eèdi*. When we feed the fire we communicate with and feed our ancestors, our departed loved ones. In this way, we remember them and respect them.

When we travel to another land, we pay the water that we travel on: *Tı Ghàts´eèdi*. We put something important to us in the water as we think about the Creator. We ask the Creator for safety in our travels. We ask non-Tłıchǫ people who travel to our lands to also pay the water to show respect for our ways and our lands.

Philip feeds the fire.

Our Traditions
Philip's Prayer to Show Thanks for Clean Water

Traditional Tłıchǫ ways of healing come from their belief in the Creator. Many Tłıchǫ, however, have accepted Christianity in addition to their belief in the old ways. While out on the land, Philip performs a service to pray for clean water:

"I'm happy this is where we get clean water. We respect the water. *Masì cho*. You are good, clear water. You are the water that everyone uses for health, for cooking, for tea, for cleaning. Help us to be in better health. *Masì cho*."

"Tı nezı̨ gha Yahtìa

Sı̨nà edı̨ı̨ ts'ǫ̀ tı at'ı̨ı̨ sì.
Tı sets'ı̨whǫ gha hǫt'è, masì cho.
Tı nezı̨ ąt'è. Nizhǫ dǫ hazhǫǫ̀ net'à at'ı̨ hǫt'e, wet'à sedèts' ewǫǫ̀, wet'à lıdì ts'ehts'ı̨, wet'à asìı hazhǫǫ̀ sets'ęwhǫ.
Gots'anedì wet'à hotıı ts'edaà.
Masì cho."

How to Make Ehgwàa

Elizabeth Chocolate's Instructions

Here Therese's son Nelson and his nephew Forest are checking the nets. They have caught several whitefish, which will be made into ehgwàa.

We also feed the fire when we are thanking the land for providing for us. We are thankful as our waters have lots of fish and we love to eat fish! My family and I set our nets in front of our community all year round. We catch and eat a lot of fish, including whitefish and lake trout, and then we make dry-fish: *ehgwàa*.

!. Scrape off the scales by running your knife against the direction of the scales.

2. Cut along the backbone so that the flesh is left on the skin.

3. Cut along the ribs so that the bones are removed.

4. Remove the head, guts, and ribs, but leave the backbone intact and leave the tail with the flesh. The backbone balances the fleshy part when it's hung to dry.

5. For a thoroughly dried fish, slice into the flesh just to the skin all along the fish. Don't cut the skin!

6. Hang the fish out to dry on poles so that smoke can reach each fish. The smoke keeps the bugs away and gives the fish a delicious flavour.

Elizabeth taught me to make ehgwàa. I have also learned other skills and about Tłįchǫ traditions and beliefs from different Elders.

Philip and his wife raised their kids on the land, as did Elizabeth and her husband. They share their skills with younger people so that they, too, can live off the land if they choose. We don't want to assume that the store will always provide for our children. We want them to be resourceful in case there is a time when they need to fend for themselves.

Philip is making a baby rattle. He has stretched scraped caribou hide over some birch wood and placed pellets from a gun inside.

Philip is teaching Bradley how to make a bow and arrow. Woodworking skills are important to know so you can build your own axe or other tools.

Elizabeth is making pounded meat. She has taken dry-meat (bogǫ̀ǫ̀) and pounded it into pieces, and she will add caribou fat and berries.

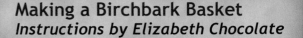

The land not only provides food but also tools for gathering food. When we are out in the bush picking berries and need a container for them, we make one.

Making a Birchbark Basket
Instructions by Elizabeth Chocolate

1. *Cut some bark from a birch tree in a way that will not kill the tree. The bigger the piece, the bigger the basket. It is easiest to have a rectangular-shaped piece. Also gather some pieces of spruce root—you'll need them later.*
2. *Warm the bark over the fire (don't burn it). Scrape all the knots off the bark and, while it's warm, make the shape you need.*
3. *Fold the corners of the bark.*
4. *You can tie a piece of string around your shape and leave it so that the bark starts to take the shape of the basket. You can also hold it in place.*
5. *Sew the spruce root into place around the rim of the basket to keep it sturdy.*

Philip shows the children how to remove the bark from the tree.

Fold it properly, and the basket will be waterproof.

The finished basket is a perfect container for picking blueberries. Activities like berry picking provide the time to share stories.

Left: In 2008, John B. Zoe received an honorary doctorate of laws from the University of Alberta. Here he is with Oree Wah-Shee, a young Tłıchǫ woman who also graduated that day with a B.A. in Native Studies.

We want our children to learn about our traditions, and we also want them to know modern ways. One of our Elders, Elizabeth Mackenzie, has a school named after her in Behchokǫ̀. She said, "If children are taught in both cultures equally, they will be strong like two people." When she said this, she was remembering the words of one of our leaders, Chief Jimmy Bruneau, who once said, "Our children will learn both ways; our way and the white man's way."

Chief Jimmy Bruneau in 1939.

The 2008 graduating class of the Chief Jimmy Bruneau high school.

Children learn how to be "strong like two people" in many ways, including listening to the old stories. Tłıchǫ stories hold our people's history and help guide how we live. Adults pass their stories along to younger people so that the stories will not be forgotten.

Philip has many stories to share. He is my husband's older brother, my Elder, and I have listened to many of his stories. Once, he told me about the place where giant animals live. We call these giant animals weyìıdìı. They live in dangerous places. The Tłıchǫ never go to these places, never, not even to this day. We show respect to the weyìıdìı and stay away.

Our Stories

One of Philip's stories about weyìidìi goes like this:

There are places where giant animals live. One such place is not far from Gamètì. Long ago, this one man, he had medicine power. He wanted to see what kind of animals lived there. He went to this place in his dreams. When he got closer, there was a big hole. In his dream he went through the hole. His children were in the hole and they were looking back at him with big, ghostlike eyes. He went back to his people and said that this is the scariest place and not to go there. To show respect you must stay away, even for hunting. If you show respect and follow the rules, weyìidìi will not harm you.

At tea break Philip shares stories with Shelinda. He has taught her how to read the land for signs of moose and other animals, how to set rabbit snares, and about where not to go.

Philip wants to share a Tłı̨chǫ story with you, but he says he's concerned about the stories being written down. It's like our stories stop living when they are put on paper. A Tłı̨chǫ story has many, many parts and no one person has the full story. To really know and use the story, and explore all of its meanings, you have to hear many versions and add your own part—that's what makes the story a living thing. We don't want the stories to ever be finished.

Philip and George Blondin are sharing stories. George is one of the North's most celebrated storytellers. He has written many books that share traditional Dene stories. He is a Member of the Order of Canada.

To help you understand the importance of Philip's story to the Tłı̨chǫ people, you need to know a little bit about *Yamǫ̀ǫzha* or "the one who travels." He is our most important cultural leader. Our Elders always tell us that when the world was new and animals and humans could change form and talk to each other, there were lots of hardships. There were giant animals that ate people. *Yamǫ̀ǫzha* made the land safe for people by killing most of the giant animals and giving us our laws. The places where these events occurred, and the stories that go with them, are sacred to us.

There is one long story that represents a single day in the life of *Yamǫ̀ǫzha* and recounts how he made the land safe and harmonious. Each place he visited became a teaching site. At the end of this long day *Yamǫ̀ǫzha* laid down to sleep. While he slept, he had a dream. Forever after, this place became a *Nàte k'è* (dreaming place). Philip shares his version of how dreaming places can help young people to know their strength and to be healthy.

Tłı̨chǫ place names are like a map. The words tell you how to get to the place. The Elders don't want people to go to important teaching sites unless they are under the guidance of a knowledgeable person. For this reason, the place names are not given in this book. Tłı̨chǫ children should go and ask an Elder for more details about these stories.

Tłı̨chǫ artist Archie Beaulieu's interpretation of Yamǫ̀ǫzha.

POWERFUL MAGIC.

ARCHIE BEAULIEU.07 N.T.

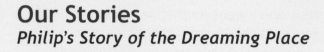

Our Stories
Philip's Story of the Dreaming Place

Once there was a boy who was born without any medicine powers, and his parents were very worried about him. He grew up without many skills. He was old enough to be on his own, but he was still relying on his parents to take care of him. They wanted him to have powers so that he could take care of himself when they were gone. They had tried many things to give him powers, the power to survive on his own. But they did not succeed.

There is a very powerful place where you go only if you want to receive medicine power. If a young person wants power, he should go and sleep there. It is a powerful place because if you don't follow what you learn there, bad things can happen. It is a drastic measure to take the chance to go to there. Even to this day people are respectful of this place and don't go there unless they are prepared to follow what they learn there.

This boy, who was now a man in age but not ability, wanted the power, medicine power. He wanted someone to go with him to this special place. He kept asking his friends over and over. Finally one of his friends agreed to go with him. Before they went, the boy's elderly father told him a story. He told him that he was to sleep at this dreaming place and when he woke up he was not to tell anyone about his dreams.

The two young men travelled to and slept there and had dreams. In the morning they woke up and asked each other, "Did anything happen?" "Did you get power?" They both answered, "Yes."

The one young man who was reluctant to go got power. He got a bow and arrow in his dreams.

He was given the power to hunt well and to help his people by providing food. He was told in his dreams that his skills with the bow and arrow were to be used for good and not to hurt people. He did not tell anyone about his dreams.

The other young man, the one who really had wanted to go, got even more power. He was given a pair of moccasins in his dreams. These moccasins were powerful, and he was told he could help heal people. In his dream he was told not to use his power until he had another dream. He went around telling people about how much power he had now.

There was a sick lady. Everyone who had power was trying to help her, but she was still very sick. The people went to the young man who had got the moccasin power and said, "Now that you have power, use it. Since you say you are so powerful, show us."

He agreed to help the lady.

He asked the lady how she wanted help. She wanted him to swallow her illness, so that is what he did. He started to sing and put his hand on her head. His whole body was shaking. He took the illness from her mouth, and instead of throwing it in the fire, he swallowed it. He died as soon as he swallowed it.

Out here on our land we have everything. People who aren't from here might look at our lands and think they are empty, but we do not go hungry. The land gives us our food and our shelter. It holds our stories and our histories. It gives us everything we need. Thanks to the sharing of our Elders, we all feel at home here.

Right: Philip teaches Shelinda to read the signs of the land. Here he is showing her where a moose has nibbled on the end of a tree branch.

We really respect our old-time Tłı̨chǫ stories. The stories contain our laws and they teach us how to live. They are very precious to us.

Philip is over eighty years old and his days are short. You young people have many years ahead of you. He says the more campfires you listen in at, the more you will know.

He does not want the stories to go to waste but for you to use them well. The story Philip shared is so sacred to him that he would only tell us part of it today. But, he wants you to think about what you have learned from the stories and about our people.

Masì.

All the Details!

ancestral trails – traditional trails along waterways that Tłįchǫ people have used for a long time to travel to places where they harvest food.

Behchokǫ̀ – a Tłįchǫ community.

bogǫǫ̀ – dry-meat.

Chief Mǫnfwì (1866-1936) – Through Mǫnfwì's leadership, the Tłįchǫ people claimed hunting and trapping rights from Fort Providence along the Mackenzie River to Great Bear Lake and across to Contwoyto Lake to present day Lutsel'ke and along the northern shore of Great Slave Lake back to Fort Providence. This area is called "Mǫnfwì Lands"—see the map on page vi. He signed Treaty 11 in 1921.

Chief Jimmy Bruneau (1881-1975) – Jimmy Bruneau succeeded Mǫnfwì as chief in 1936. He understood that times were changing and that people needed both their traditional knowledge and that which they could learn in school.

Dogrib - The English name for the Tłįchǫ people and language. The Dogrib or Tłįchǫ language is in a close family of about thirty languages called Na-Dene or Athapaskan.

drum-dance - a traditional Tłįchǫ dance.

edàt'e – How are you?

ehgwàa – dry-fish, often made of whitefish and lake trout.

ehtsèe – grandfather.

fast (as in a health fast) - used by some when they want to heal. To do so, they do not eat for a period of time to cleanse their bodies and minds.

feeding the fire (Kǫ̀ Ghàts' eèdi) – giving gifts, such as tea, bannock, or dry-meat, to a fire in order to communicate with and feed ancestors.

Gamètì – a Tłįchǫ community and home to Therese Zoe, Philip Zoe, and their families.

George Blondin - a Tłįchǫ storyteller and author. His books include: When the World Was New, Yamoria the Lawmaker, and Trail of the Spirit.

Ịdaà Trail – a waterway and ancestral trail that connects Great Slave Lake to Great Bear Lake.

In the Trails of Our Ancestors – the name of the journeys made by boat to the Tłįchǫ gatherings that happen every summer.

land claim - an agreement that is recognized in the Canadian constitution between an Aboriginal group and the government of Canada. The Tłįchǫ Land Claims and Self-government Agreement was signed on Aug 25, 2003, exactly eighty-two years after Treaty 11 was signed by Chief Mǫnfwì.

Masì Cho – Thank you very much.

medicine person (Ịk'ǫǫ̀ dǫ) - a traditional doctor in the Tłįchǫ community who has healing power.

Nàte K'è – a "dreaming place".

paying the water (Tı Ghàts' eèdi) – placing something important in the water that is travelled on, to show respect for the Creator and to ask for safety in travels.

rat root (dzǫdìı) – a powerful plant that helps people when they travel, and with ailments like headaches and stomachaches.

sweat lodge - a ceremonial sauna that helps heal minds and bodies.

tea dance - a traditional Tłįchǫ circle dance wherein there are no drums and only male singers.

treaty – a formal agreement between an Aboriginal people and the government of Canada. Today treaties are called land claims. Tłįchǫ Chief Mǫnfwì signed Treaty 11 with the Canadian government in 1921.

Wekwetì – a Tłįchǫ community.

weyììdìı – giant animals.

Whatì – a Tłįchǫ community.

Yamǫǫzha – (known by different names) the most important Tłįchǫ cultural leader who made the world safe and gave all Dene people, including the Tłįchǫ, their laws.

Tłįchǫ Stories

Learning Place Names and Stories from Elders – Stories originate in places where people have experiences that teach them to live correctly. Place names and stories are best learned from Elders. People should visit some places with greater understanding and sensitivity; they must know how to behave at these places. The Regional Elders' Committee, of which Philip Zoe is a member, expect youth to demonstrate an understanding of a place's significance before they visit it. Learning about and visiting should be done under the guidance of an Elder. The Elders want young people to learn what a significant place name represents. For this reason, the stories in this book are without place names, without the mental map that place names provide. Rather young people are encouraged to learn the names of these places and the Tłįchǫ principles attached to these place names from their Elders. (Madelaine Chocolate and Allice Legat)

Living Stories – According to John B. Zoe, Tłįchǫ stories are alive because the person who tells them makes them relevant to the person listening. The storyteller changes the details of the story to make it fit the purpose. Each story has a few points that stay the same.
  For example, in Philip's story, the following things remain the same no matter who is telling the story:
- Young man cannot survive by himself and needs a dream to help.
- Elder leads young man to the dreaming place to sleep.
- Young man is told what to expect and to be respectful of self.
- Young man ignores what he was told.
- Young man dies.

To illustrate the way Tlicho stories live in the Tłįchǫ culture, John B. Zoe's version (he heard it from Harry Simpson and Nick Black) is included here:

> Once there was a young man still living with his elderly parents who wanted him to be able to have skills of his own. They were worried about him because they knew they did not have long to live and their son could still not take care of himself. Because there wasn't much time, they had to take drastic measures. The father wanted the boy to acquire knowledge to survive on the land, and so he decided to take his son to a dreaming place.
>
> They climbed a mountain and before the young man went to sleep, the father told him a story of what would happen.
>
> The father told his son that he would fall asleep and in his dream he would be given a cup. He said, "You are only to drink what you need and give the cup back. Don't talk to anyone about your dreams until they have come true."
>
> The young boy went to sleep and in his dream he was given a cup. In his dream he gulped it all down and threw the cup back. When he woke up he started talking about his dream. As he walked down the mountain, he told his father everything. When he went to bed that night, he didn't wake up.

Tłįchǫ Community Services Agency (TCSA) - The vision statement of TCSA is "Strong Like Two People." In 1971, Chief Jimmy Bruneau officially opened the school that was to bear his name. On this occasion, he spoke of the importance of biculturalism and bilingual education, where equal emphasis would be given to educating children in two cultures. Go to www.tlicho.ca to learn more.

About the Authors and Photographer

Therese Zoe is the daughter of Adele and Alphonse Wedawin. She is married to Louis Zoe and they have five children; Kevin, Sally, Francis, Nancy, and Nelson. She has eight grandchildren including Francis's children, whom you met in this story. She is very proud of her language and culture and hopes that the stories shared here will assist young Tłı̨chǫ to learn more about their culture. She also hopes all Canadians will learn and respect the Tłı̨chǫ ways.

Philip Zoe is a respected Elder from Gamètì. His wife, Bella, passed away two years ago. Together they raised four children, Peter, Camilla, Alice, and Bobby, and they have ten grandchildren. Philip gets up early in the morning, works hard all day, and always thanks the land for what it offers. He is very fit from a lifetime of living on the land. Even though he is 82 years old, young people still have a hard time keeping up with him in the bush. Philip starred in an award-winning documentary called *My Land is My Life*.

Mindy Willett is an educator from Yellowknife, NWT. After working with Therese and Philip on this book, she was inspired to paddle from Gamètì south to Yellowknife on the Ɂdaà Trail with her young family. She's very thankful for the generosity of the Tłı̨chǫ people in sharing their land and stories and will soon paddle from Gamètì north to Great Bear Lake to visit the other places in the stories told by Philip and Therese.

Tessa Macintosh worked as a photographer for Native Press and the NWT government for many years. She is now a freelance photographer living in Yellowknife. One of her career highlights was photographing the Trails of Our Ancestor's canoe trip and producing a book by the same title. This region has a special place in her heart because her children are Tłı̨chǫ.